Persian Cookbook

A Persian Cookbook Filled with Authentic Persian Recipes for Easy Persian Cooking At Home

By
BookSumo Press
All rights reserved

Published by
http://www.booksumo.com

ENJOY THE RECIPES?

KEEP ON COOKING WITH 6 MORE FREE COOKBOOKS!

Visit our website and simply enter your email address to join the club and receive your 6 cookbooks.

http://booksumo.com/magnet

https://www.instagram.com/booksumopress/

https://www.facebook.com/booksumo/

LEGAL NOTES

All Rights Reserved. No Part Of This Book May Be Reproduced Or Transmitted In Any Form Or By Any Means. Photocopying, Posting Online, And / Or Digital Copying Is Strictly Prohibited Unless Written Permission Is Granted By The Book's Publishing Company. Limited Use Of The Book's Text Is Permitted For Use In Reviews Written For The Public.

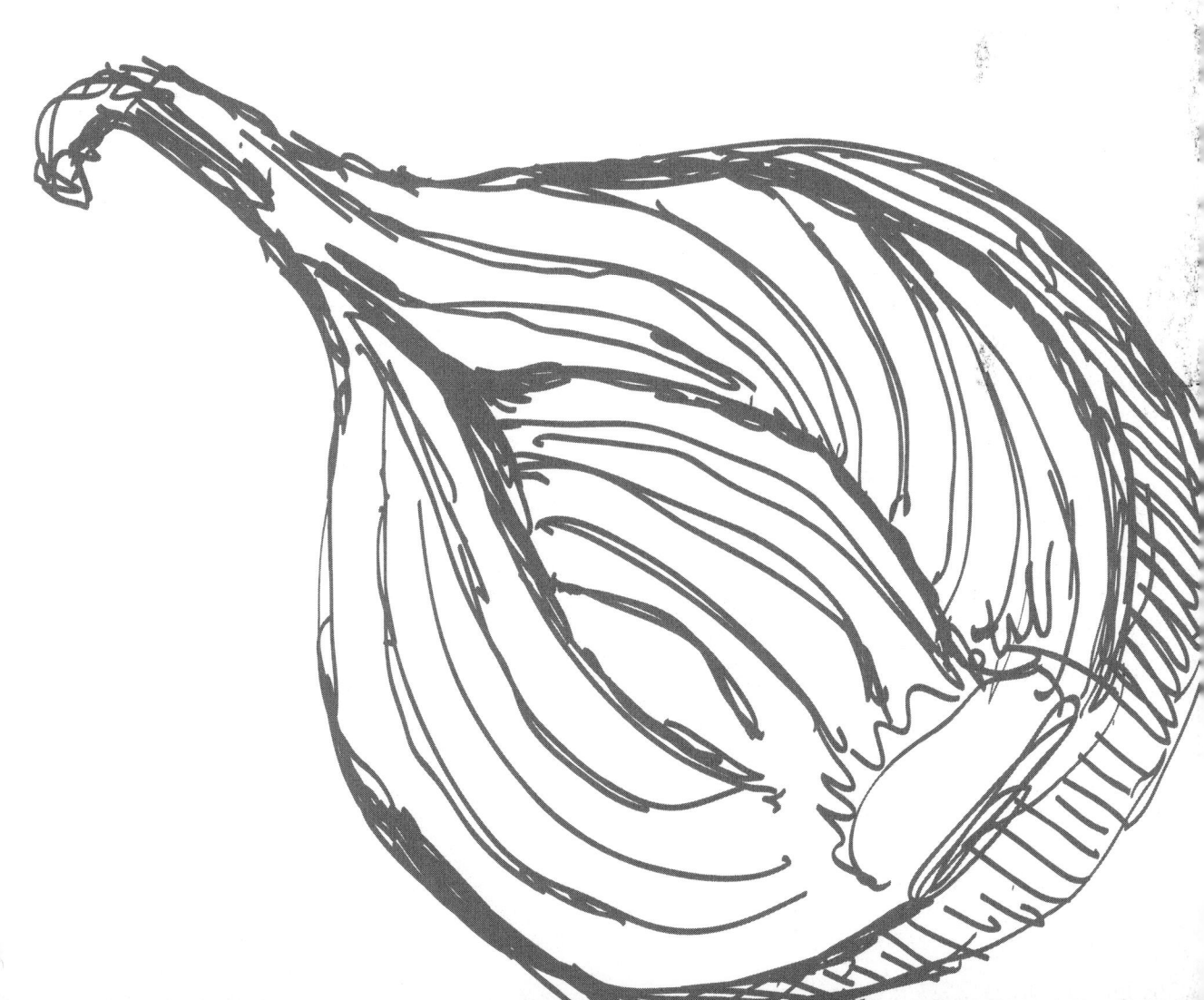

Table of Contents

Persian Orange and Bean Stew 7

Persian Potato Rice Stew 8

Persian Nutty Rice 9

Persian Pistachios and Bean Pilaf 10

Persian Noodles Bean Soup 11

Persian Lemon Chicken Kabobs 13

Persian Chicken Wings Soup 14

Potato and Pepper Meatballs 15

Persian Chicken Berries Pilaf 16

Persian Lime Lamb Stew 17

Persian Zucchini Frittata 18

Persian Spinach Frittata 19

Glazed Lamb with Fruit Salad 20

Persian Creamy Dill Chicken Salad 21

Persian Saffron Kabobs 22

Persian Tongues Stew 23

Persian Lentils and Meatballs Soup 24

Persian Eggplant Frittata 25

Persian Nutty Duck 26

Persian Nutty Fruit Salad 27

Persian Nutty Yogurt Soup 28

Persian Rosy Rice Pudding 29

Fenugreek Lamb Stew 30
Persian Cinnamon Beef Stew 31
Persian Lemon Kabobs 32
Persian Potato Lamb Stew 33
Persian Allspice Fish Fillets 34
Persian Meaty Okra Lime Stew 35
Persian Basmati Chicken Casserole 36
Persian Lemon Linguini 37
Persian Herbed Rice 38
Persian Kashk Lamb Meatballs Stew 39
Persian Sesame Bread 40
Persian Kings' Almond Lamb Stew 41
Chicken Apricots Stir Fry 42
Persian Potato Frittata 43
Persian Cinnamon Basmati Pilaf 44
Persian Walnuts Cake 45
Persian Valentine Almond Cake 46
Persian Basmati Prunes Soup 47
Persian Orangy Nuts Soup 48
Persian Yogurt Beef Soup 49
Persian Garbanzo Soup 50
Persian Lover's Rose Tea 51
Persian Beef Pasta Sauce 52
Persian Herbed Cucumber Cream Dip 53

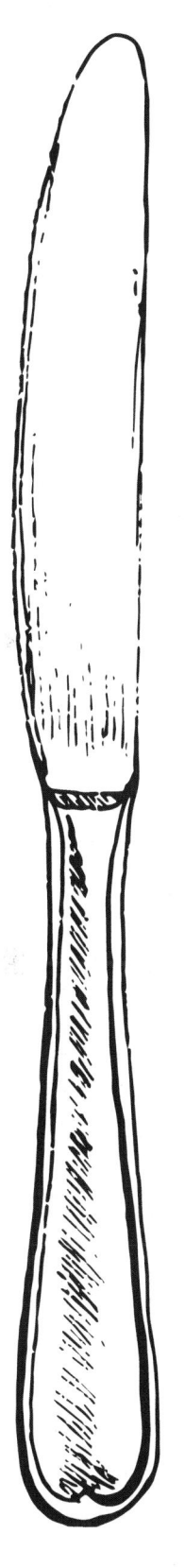

Creamy Roasted Persian Eggplant Lime Dip 54
Creamy Persian Zesty Garlic Dip 55
Persian Greek Dip 56
Grilled Persian Garlic and Eggplant Dip 57
Refreshing Nutty Cucumber Cream Salad 58

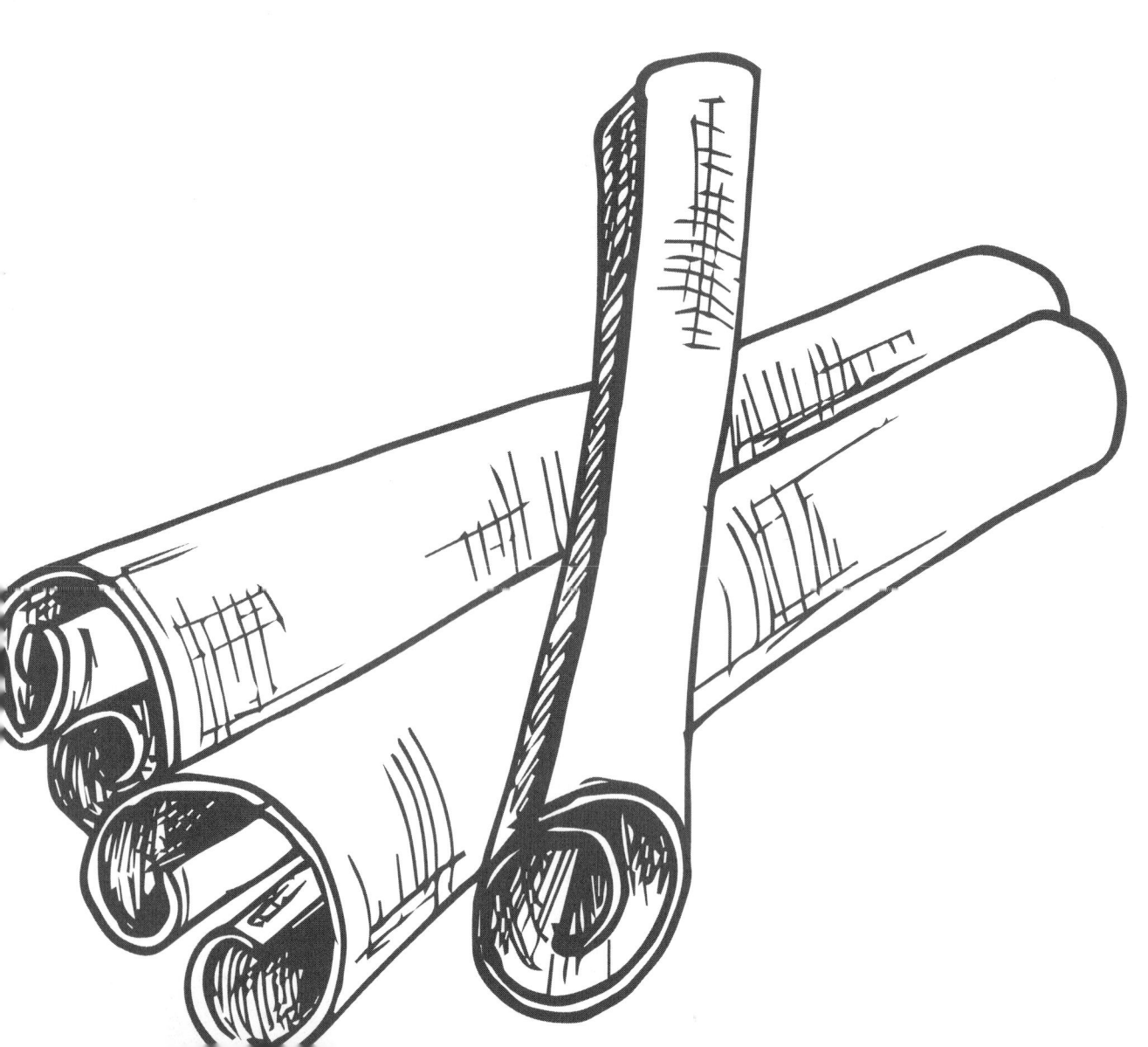

Persian Orange and Bean Stew

Prep Time: 12 mins
Total Time: 15 mins

Servings per Recipe: 4
Calories	493.2
Fat	6.5g
Cholesterol	0.0mg
Sodium	2222.4mg
Carbohydrates	85.6g
Protein	26.1g

Ingredients

- 1 tbsp olive oil
- 2 onions, chopped
- 3 cloves garlic, chopped
- 1 tsp salt
- 1 tsp cumin
- 1/4 tsp cinnamon
- 1 C. orange juice
- 1 lime, juice of
- 1 can tomato paste
- 4 (15 1/2 oz.) cans kidney beans, rinsed and drained
- 1 jalapeno, chopped
- pita bread

Directions

1. Place a large skillet over medium heat. Heat the oil in it. Add the onion and cook it for 6 min.
2. Stir in the spices and cook them for another 6 min. Add the orange and lime juice. Cook them until they start boiling. Cook them for 12 min over low heat.
3. Stir in the peppers with beans. Cook them for 22 min. cook them for 5 min. serve your stew warm.
4. Enjoy.

PERSIAN
Potato Rice Stew

Prep Time: 3 hrs
Total Time: 3 hrs 45 mins

Servings per Recipe: 6
Calories	499.7
Fat	9.7g
Cholesterol	0.0mg
Sodium	11.4mg
Carbohydrates	92.5g
Protein	8.7g

Ingredients

- 3 C. of white long grain rice
- 4 tbsp cooking oil
- 3 - 4 medium potatoes
- 4 oz. water
- salt

Directions

1. Get a large bowl: Place in it the rice and cover it with hot water and a pinch of salt. Place it aside.
2. Remove the peel of the potato and slice them.
3. Place a medium pot and fill half of it with water. Place in it the rice and cook it until it starts boiling. Once the rice is half done drain it.
4. Place a large pot over medium heat. Heat the oil in it. Stir in the water. Spread the potato in the pot and sprinkle on it some sat. Top it with rice.
5. Make a hole in the center of the rice layer and another 4 holes on the side. Drizzle some water on top. Put on the lid and cook them for 3 min over high heat.
6. Lower the heat and drizzle some oil top. Lower the heat to medium heat and cook it for 16 min.
7. Lower the heat to medium low. Drizzle more of some oil on top then cook it for 12 min. serve your potato rice warm.
8. Enjoy.

Persian Nutty Rice

Prep Time: 10 mins
Total Time: 35 mins

Servings per Recipe: 4
Calories   280.1
Fat   9.7g
Cholesterol   15.2mg
Sodium   373.5mg
Carbohydrates   44.2g
Protein   5.2g

Ingredients

2 tbsp butter
1 C. white basmati rice, rinsed under cold water in a fine mesh sieve
1/2 tsp salt
1/4 tsp cracked black pepper
1 garlic clove, minced
orange peel
1/2 tsp ground cinnamon
1/4 tsp curry powder
2 C. water
3 tbsp roasted pistachios
3 tbsp golden raisins

Directions

1. Place a large skillet over medium heat. Stir in it the rice for 5 min while stirring it.
2. Add the salt, pepper, garlic, orange peel, cinnamon and curry powder. Cook them for 2 min. Stir in the water and put on the lid. Lower the heat.
3. Cook them for 26 min. Place the cover aside and add to it the pistachios and golden raisins. Discard the orange peel. Serve your nutty rice warm.
4. Enjoy.

PERSIAN Pistachios and Bean Pilaf

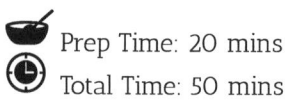

Prep Time: 20 mins
Total Time: 50 mins

Servings per Recipe: 4
Calories 411.0
Fat 15.6g
Cholesterol 0.0mg
Sodium 215.8mg
Carbohydrates 56.2g
Protein 15.4g

Ingredients

150 g frozen broad beans
1 tbsp olive oil
1 large kumara, peeled, cut into 2cm cubes (orange sweet potato)
1 brown onion, finely chopped
2 tsp finely grated ginger
1 tsp ground cumin
1 tsp ground coriander
1 tsp ground turmeric
1 tsp ground paprika
190 g quinoa, rinsed, drained
500 ml vegetable stock
1 bunch kale, stems trimmed, shredded
75 g pistachios, toasted, coarsely chopped
1/2 C. coriander leaves
lemon wedge, to serve

Directions

1. Before you do anything preheat the oven to 400 F. Cover a baking sheet with a piece of parchment paper.
2. Lay the kumara in the baking sheet and drizzle some of the oil on it. Sprinkle some salt and pepper on it. Cook it in the oven for 22 min.
3. Bring a large saucepan of water to a boil. Add the broad beans and cook it 3 min. Drain it and rinse it with cool water. Remove the broad bean peel.
4. Place a large saucepan over medium heat. Heat the rest of the oil in it. Sauté in it the onion for 6 min.
5. Stir in the ginger, cumin, coriander, turmeric and paprika. Sauté them for 2 min.
6. Combine the stock with quinoa in a large saucepan. Cook them until they start boiling. Lower the heat and put on the lid. Cook them for 16 min.
7. Add the kale and cook them for 2 min. Stir in the kumara, broad beans and pistachios, salt and pepper. Serve your Pilaf warm.
8. Enjoy.

Persian Noodles Bean Soup

Prep Time: 2 hrs
Total Time: 3 hrs 47 mins

Servings per Recipe: 8
Calories   414.9
Fat   23.5g
Cholesterol   2.7mg
Sodium   563.9mg
Carbohydrates   43.8g
Protein   11.7g

Ingredients

- 100 g chickpeas
- 100 g lentils
- 100 g navy beans or 100 g kidney beans
- 250 g flat wheat noodles
- 1/2 C. closely packed fresh coriander, finely chopped
- 1/2 C. closely packed fresh spinach, finely chopped
- 1/2 C. closely packed fresh chives, finely chopped
- 1/2 C. closely packed fresh dill, finely chopped (tips)
- 1/2 C. closely packed fresh parsley, finely chopped
- 1/2 C. oil
- 3 tbsp plain flour
- 1 C. buttermilk
- 2 tbsp sour cream
- 1/2 tsp turmeric
- 1/2 tsp ground black pepper, to taste
- 100 g walnuts (kernels)
- 1/4 C. crushed dried mint
- 1/2 tbsp salt, to taste
- 4 medium onions
- 6 C. water
- 9 C. water
- 1/2 C. water

Directions

1. Soak the chickpeas in some water for 2 h 30 min. Place a large pot over medium heat. Pour 6 C. of water in the pot. Add the chickpeas and cook it for 45 min.
2. Clean the lentils with some water. Stir them into the pot and cook them for 25 min while stirring often. Clean it.
3. Clean the herbs with some water and dry them.
4. Place a large pan over medium heat. Heat 1/4 C. oil in it. Chop the onion and cook in it for 6 min. Place half of it aside. Stir in the turmeric and cook them for 2 min.
5. Stir the cooked turmeric onion with 9 C. of water and noodles. Cook them for 6 min.
6. Whisk half C. of water with flour until they become smooth. Stir it with the chopped herbs into the pot. Lower the heat and cook them for 42 min.

7. Add the buttermilk with sour cream. Cook them for 3 min.
8. Heat 1/4 C. of oil in it in a large pan. Cook in it the dry mint for 2 min. Serve your soup hot with the dried mint warm.
9. Enjoy.

Persian Lemon Chicken Kabobs

Prep Time: 10 mins
Total Time: 40 mins

Servings per Recipe: 4
Calories   432.4
Fat   33.7g
Cholesterol   92.8mg
Sodium   673.4mg
Carbohydrates   1.1g
Protein   30.3g

Ingredients

- 4 boneless chicken breasts, cut in cubes
- 6 tbsp olive oil
- 1/16 tsp saffron, crushed
- 3 tbsp lemon juice
- 1 tsp salt
- 1/4 tsp pepper
- 1/4 tsp basil
- 1/4 tsp turmeric
- 1/4 tsp garlic powder

Directions

1. Get a large mixing bowl: Stir into it all the ingredients. Place it in the fridge for 2 h 30 min.
2. Preheat the grill and grease its grates.
3. Thread the chicken pieces into skewers and cook them on the grill for 35 min while turning them often. Serve your kabobs warm.
4. Enjoy.

PERSIAN Chicken Wings Soup

Prep Time: 20 mins
Total Time: 1 hr 30 mins

Servings per Recipe: 6
Calories 656.2
Fat 36.0g
Cholesterol 165.3mg
Sodium 934.2mg
Carbohydrates 34.0g
Protein 47.9g

Ingredients

1/4 C. canola oil
1 lb chicken wings
kosher salt & freshly ground black pepper, to taste
3 medium onions (2 roughly chopped, 1 minced)
3 medium carrots, roughly chopped
2 garlic cloves, crushed
8 C. chicken stock
1 bay leaf
1 1/2 lbs ground chicken
1 1/2 C. chickpea flour
2 1/2 tsp ground turmeric
2 tsp ground coriander
1 1/2 tsp baking soda
1/2 tsp ground cardamom

Directions

1. Place a soup pot over medium heat. Heat 3 tbsp of oil in it.
2. Sprinkle some salt and pepper over the chicken wings. Brown it in the pot for 14 min. Stir in the onions, carrots, and garlic. Sauté them for 10 min.
3. Stir in the stock, bay leaf, and salt. Cook them until they start boiling. Lower the heat and cook the soup for 37 min.
4. Pour the broth in a colander and drain it. Discard the chicken wings with veggies. Pour the broth into the pot.
5. Heat the oil in a large pan. Add the onion and cook them for 5 min. Allow it to cool down slightly.
6. Get a large mixing bowl: Combine in it the rest of the ingredients and mix them well. Shape the mix into meatballs.
7. Stir the meatballs into the hot broth. Cook them until they start simmering. Put on half a cover over the pot. Cook the soup for 18 min. Serve your soup warm.
8. Enjoy.

Potato and Pepper Meatballs

Prep Time: 15 mins
Total Time: 1 hr

Servings per Recipe: 6
Calories   188.5
Fat   3.3g
Cholesterol   124.0mg
Sodium   88.8mg
Carbohydrates   32.2g
Protein   7.9g

Ingredients

- 5 medium potatoes or 600 g potatoes
- 4 eggs
- 1 medium green bell pepper, chopped
- 1/4 tsp saffron
- salt
- pepper
- 1/2 tsp baking powder
- frying oil

Directions

1. Bring a salted pot of water to a boil. Cook in it the potato until it becomes soft. Drain it and place it aside.
2. Place the potato in a grater and grate it.
3. Get a large mixing bowl: Mix in it the potato with eggs, bell pepper, a pinch of salt and pepper. Mix them well. Add the saffron with baking powder. Mix them again.
4. Place a large skillet over medium heat. Heat the oil in it. Shape the mix into patties and cook them in the pan for 10 min on each side with the lid on.
5. Serve your potato patties warm.
6. Enjoy.

PERSIAN
Chicken Berries Pilaf

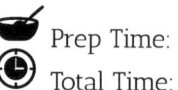

Prep Time: 15 mins
Total Time: 1 hr

Servings per Recipe: 4
Calories	1371.1
Fat	77.8g
Cholesterol	279.9mg
Sodium	567.0mg
Carbohydrates	129.0g
Protein	43.7g

Ingredients

7 oz. raisins
6 oz. barberries
6 onions, large
1/2 lb butter
salt, to taste
pepper, to taste
8 chicken thighs
2 C. basmati rice

Directions

1. Before you do anything preheat the oven to 400 F.
2. Place a large pan over medium heat. Heat 2 oz. of butter until it melts. Sprinkle some salt and pepper over the chicken thighs. Coat it with some of the melted butter.
3. Lay the chicken thighs on a lined up baking sheet. Cook it in the oven for 48 min.
4. Cut the onion into slices. Cook it in the pan with a pinch of salt for 4 min. Add the raisins with barberries. Cook them for 1 min. Turn off the heat and let the mix cool down slightly.
5. Put the chicken thighs on a serving plate and top them with rice and onion berries mix. Serve it warm.
6. Enjoy

Persian Lime Lamb Stew

 Prep Time: 45 mins
 Total Time: 3 hrs 15 mins

Servings per Recipe: 6
Calories   244.3
Fat   15.8g
Cholesterol   48.3mg
Sodium   493.9mg
Carbohydrates   9.0g
Protein   18.2g

Ingredients

2 large onions, peeled and thinly sliced
1 lb stew meat, cut in 1-inch cubes (lamb, veal or beef)
1/3 C. oil
1 tsp salt
1/2 tsp ground black pepper
1/2 tsp turmeric

5 stalks celery, washed and cut into 1 inch lengths
3 C. chopped fresh parsley
1/2 chopped of fresh mint
1/3 C. fresh squeezed lime juice

Directions

1. Place a pot over medium heat. Add 3 tbsp of oil and heat it. Cook in it the lamb meat with onion, turmeric, a pinch of salt and pepper. Cook them for 4 min.
2. Stir in 2 C. of water. Put on the lid and cook them for 35 min.
3. Place a large pan over medium heat. Heat 3 tbsp of oil in it. Add the celery and sauté it for 12 min. Stir in the herbs and cook them for 12 min.
4. Transfer the mix to the pot with lime juice. Put on the lid and cook them for 1 h 35 min. Adjust the seasoning of the soup then serve it warm.
5. Enjoy

PERSIAN
Zucchini Frittata

Prep Time: 10 mins
Total Time: 55 mins

Servings per Recipe: 6
Calories   80.1
Fat   3.5g
Cholesterol   141.0mg
Sodium   160.6mg
Carbohydrates   7.2g
Protein   5.5g

Ingredients

2 medium onions, chopped
4 garlic cloves, minced
1 lb zucchini, grated
4 eggs
1/2 tsp turmeric

1/2 tsp baking soda
salt and pepper
olive oil
cooking spray

Directions

1. Place a large pan over medium heat. Heat the oil in it. Sauté in it the turmeric with onion for 3 min.
2. Add the zucchini with a pinch of salt and pepper. Cook them for 4 min.
3. Get a large mixing bowl: Beat the eggs in it. Add the baking soda with a pinch of salt and pepper. Whisk them again. Fold in the onion and zucchini mix.
4. Before you do anything preheat the oven to 375 F.
5. Pour the mix into a greased baking dish. Cook it in the oven for 35 min. Serve it warm.
6. Enjoy.

Persian Spinach Frittata

Prep Time: 10 mins
Total Time: 30 mins

Servings per Recipe: 3
Calories   328.1
Fat   20.2g
Cholesterol   423.0mg
Sodium   769.3mg
Carbohydrates   19.2g
Protein   21.9g

Ingredients

- 2 lbs fresh baby spinach leaves
- 1/4 C. water
- 2 tbsp oil
- 2 medium onions, sliced thin (1 C.)
- 1/2 tsp salt (to taste)
- 1/8 tsp ground turmeric
- 1/8 tsp pepper
- 6 eggs

Directions

1. Pour 1/4 C. of water in a medium sauce. Pour into it 1/4 C. of water in it. Put on the lid and cook them for 6 min. Turn off the heat and let the spinach sit for 6 min.
2. Drain the spinach and squeeze it from the water.
3. Place a large pan over medium heat. Heat the oil in it. Add the onion with turmeric, a pinch of salt and pepper. Cook them for 4 min.
4. Stir in the spinach for 4 min. Make 6 holes in them. Crack an egg in each hole. Cook them for 6 min over low heat until the eggs are done. Serve your skillet warm.
5. Enjoy.

GLAZED Lamb with Fruit Salad

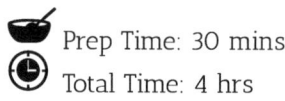

Prep Time: 30 mins
Total Time: 4 hrs

Servings per Recipe: 6
Calories 95.5
Fat 4.8g
Cholesterol 0.0mg
Sodium 10.6mg
Carbohydrates 14.4g
Protein 1.4g

Ingredients

4 tbsp pomegranate molasses
1 tsp ground cumin
1 lemon, juice of
1 tbsp olive oil
2 garlic cloves, minced
1 onion, roughly chopped
1 lamb shoulder, weighing about 1.6kg, lightly scored

2 pomegranates, seeds only
handful flat leaf parsley
100 g watercress
1 small red onion, finely diced
1 tbsp olive oil
flat bread, to serve

Directions

1. Before you do anything preheat the oven to 320 F.
2. Get a small mixing bowl: Stir in it the molasses with the cumin, lemon juice, olive oil and garlic to make the sauce.
3. Spread the onion in a greased casserole dish. Place the lamb on it and pour the sauce all over it. Pour 3/4 over the lamb mix.
4. Place a large piece of foil over the casserole dish. Cook it in the oven for 3 h 30 min.
5. Toss the red onion with pomegranate and olive oil in a large salad bowl. Serve it with the roasted lamb warm.
6. Enjoy.

Persian Creamy Dill Chicken Salad

Prep Time: 10 mins
Total Time: 1 hr 10 mins

Servings per Recipe: 6
Calories 268.4
Fat 8.4g
Cholesterol 124.7mg
Sodium 842.5mg
Carbohydrates 35.4g
Protein 13.0g

Ingredients

- 5 white potatoes
- 3 dill pickles
- 1 onion, halved
- 1 1/2 C. green peas, frozen
- 3 carrots, peeled
- 1 chicken breast
- 3 eggs
- 4 tbsp white vinegar
- 4 tbsp light mayonnaise
- 1/2 tsp turmeric
- salt and pepper

Directions

1. Pour 2 C. of water in a pot and cook it until it starts boiling. Add the chicken breast, onion, carrots, turmeric, and some salt. Cook them for 50 min. Allow the mix to cool down.
2. Drain the onion and discard it. Drain the chicken and shred it. Place it aside. Dice the carrots and place them aside.
3. Combine the potato with eggs in another pot and cover them with water. Cook them for 14 min. Peel the eggs and place them aside. Peel the potatoes and dice them. Dice the pickles.
4. Get a large mixing bowl: Toss in it the potatoes, chicken, carrots, pickles, peas, and eggs.
5. Get a small mixing bowl: Mix in it the vinegar with mayonnaise, a pinch of salt and pepper. Add the mix to the veggies and chicken. Serve your salad.
6. Enjoy.

PERSIAN
Saffron Kabobs

Prep Time: 20 mins
Total Time: 40 mins

Servings per Recipe: 8
Calories	185.7
Fat	9.4g
Cholesterol	101.5mg
Sodium	387.0mg
Carbohydrates	1.9g
Protein	23.4g

Ingredients

2 lbs lean ground turkey
1 medium onion
1 egg
1 tbsp dried dill
1 tbsp dried coriander
1 tsp cumin
1 tsp sea salt
1/2 tsp pepper

1/4 tsp cayenne pepper
1/4 tsp turmeric
1/4 tsp saffron thread
1 pinch salt

Directions

1. Grate the onion in a grater. Squeeze it from the liquid.
2. Get a large mixing bowl: Toss in it the turkey, grated onion, egg, and remaining spices, except for the saffron threads.
3. Place a large pan over medium heat. Cook in it the saffron with a pinch of salt. Cook them for 10 sec. Transfer it to a mortar and grind it. Stir it into the turkey mix.
4. Mix them well. Place the mix in the fridge for an overnight.
5. Shape the mix into 8 or 10 logs and press them into the skewers. Place them in the fridge for an hour or more.
6. Preheat the oven broiler. Place the skewers on a roasting pan and cook them in the oven for 10 min on each side. Serve them warm.
7. Enjoy.

Persian Tongues Stew

Prep Time: 5 mins
Total Time: 5 hrs 5 mins

Servings per Recipe: 4
Calories   232.5
Fat   20.9g
Cholesterol   53.4mg
Sodium   208.4mg
Carbohydrates   10.0g
Protein   4.9g

Ingredients

- 1 beef tongue
- 1 sheep tongue
- 2 - 3 garlic cloves
- 1 medium onion
- 3 - 4 tsp tomato paste
- 500 g mushrooms
- 100 g butter
- 200 g parsley (ends)
- salt
- black pepper

Directions

1. Clean the beef and sheep tongues well with cool water.
2. Place them in a large soup pot. Cover them with hot water. Cook them until foam start rising on top.
3. Slice the garlic and onion then add them to the pot. Chop the herbs and add them to the pot with some salt and peppers.
4. Cook them over low heat for 4 h 30 min. Peel the tongues and remove their skin. Slice them.
5. Place a large pan over medium heat. Melt the butter in it. Slice the mushroom and cook it in it for 4 min. Add the tomato paste with the rest of the liquid from the tongues pot.
6. Cook them until they start boiling. Keep cooking them for 3 min. Pour the mix all over the slices tongues and serve them warm.
7. Enjoy.

PERSIAN
Lentils and Meatballs Soup

 Prep Time: 20 mins
Total Time: 1 hr 20 mins

Servings per Recipe: 6
Calories   145.6
Fat   6.1g
Cholesterol   31.0mg
Sodium   811.2mg
Carbohydrates   11.9g
Protein   10.6g

Ingredients

SOUP
1/4 C. lentils
1/4 C. dried black-eyed peas
4 -5 C. water
1 1/2 tsp salt
1 C. fine egg noodles
1/2 C. chopped parsley
MEATBALLS
1/2 lb ground beef
1/3 C. finely chopped onions or 1/3 C. grated onion

1/4 tsp cinnamon
1/4 tsp fine grind black pepper
1/2 tsp salt
SPICE GARNISH
2 tsp dried mint
1/2 tsp black pepper
1/4 tsp cinnamon

Directions

1. Place a large pot of water over medium heat with a pinch of salt. Cook in it the beans with lentils for 38 min. Stir in the parsley with noodles.
2. Get a large mixing bowl: Combine in it the meatballs ingredients and mix them well. Shape the mix into meatballs. Add them to the pot and cook them for 35 min.
3. Get a mortar: Crush in it the mint with cinnamon and pepper. Sprinkle it over the soup then serve it warm.
4. Enjoy.

Persian Eggplant Frittata

Prep Time: 15 mins
Total Time: 1 hr 25 mins

Servings per Recipe: 4
Calories 432.0
Fat 32.8g
Cholesterol 211.5mg
Sodium 766.5mg
Carbohydrates 27.5g
Protein 11.2g

Ingredients

2 large eggplants or 6 small eggplants, peeled and cut into thin strips
1 egg white, lightly beaten
1/2 C. vegetable oil, butter or 1/2 C. ghee
2 large onions, peeled and thinly sliced
4 garlic cloves, peeled and crushed
4 eggs
4 tbsp chopped fresh parsley
1/4 tsp powdered saffron, dissolved in 1 tbsp hot water
1 lime, juice of

1 tsp baking powder
1 tbsp all-purpose flour
1 tsp salt
1/4 tsp fresh ground black pepper

Directions

1. Remove the peel of the eggplants. Season them with some salt. Slice them into lengthwise. Brush both sides of the eggplant with the white egg.
2. Place a large pan over medium heat. Heat 4 tbsp of oil in it. Cook in it the onion for 12 min. Cook in it the garlic with eggplant for 12 min.
3. Before you do anything preheat the oven to 350 F.
4. Line up a baking dish with a parchment paper. Spread in the bottom of it 4 tbsp of vegetable oil.
5. Get a large mixing bowl: Whisk in it the eggs. Combine in it the parsley, saffron water, lime juice, baking powder, flour, salt, and pepper. Mix them well.
6. Combine the eggplant, onion and garlic. Stir them well. Cook them for 48 min. Serve your frittata warm.
7. Enjoy.

PERSIAN
Nutty Duck

🥣 Prep Time: 30 mins
⏲ Total Time: 1 hr 30 mins

Servings per Recipe: 4
Calories 1396.2
Fat 131.3g
Cholesterol 240.9mg
Sodium 204.6mg
Carbohydrates 13.9g
Protein 38.5g

Ingredients

1 duck, cut into quarters
2 onions, sliced
10 oz. finely chopped walnuts
2 1/2 C. water
salt and pepper, to taste

4 tbsp pomegranate syrup
2 tbsp sugar
2 tbsp lemon juice

Directions

1. Sprinkle some salt and pepper over the duck.
2. Place a large stew pot over medium heat. Melt in it the duck fat. Brown in it the duck pieces for 5 min. Add the onion and cook it for 3 min.
3. Remove the duck pieces from the pot and place them aside. Stir in the walnuts with 2 1/2 C. of water, a pinch of salt and pepper. Cook them for 1 min.
4. Stir in back the duck pieces. Cook them until they start boiling. Lower the heat and cook them for 1 h 10 min.
5. Get a small mixing bowl: Whisk in it the pomegranate syrup and sugar with the lemon juice. Spoon the fat from the rose on top and discard it.
6. Lower the heat and cook it for 32 min. Serve it warm.
7. Enjoy.

Persian
Nutty Fruit Salad

Prep Time: 5 mins
Total Time: 5 mins

Servings per Recipe: 6
Calories	442.5
Fat	12.7g
Cholesterol	0.0mg
Sodium	82.8mg
Carbohydrates	84.2g
Protein	8.1g

Ingredients

- 2 seedless oranges, peeled and cored
- 2 apples, peeled and cored
- 2 bananas, sliced
- 2 C. pitted dates, chopped
- 1 C. dried figs, chopped or 1 C. apricot
- 1 C. orange juice
- 1 C. almonds, chopped or 1 C. shredded coconut

Directions

1. Get a large mixing bowl: Stir in it the oranges with apples, bananas, dates and figs.
2. Pour the orange juice all over it and mix it well. Top it with almonds then place it in the fridge until ready to serve.
3. Enjoy.

PERSIAN
Nutty Yogurt Soup

🥣 Prep Time: 10 mins
🕐 Total Time: 10 mins

Servings per Recipe: 6
Calories   110.9
Fat   5.4g
Cholesterol   21.2mg
Sodium   77.2mg
Carbohydrates   10.3g
Protein   6.2g

Ingredients

32 fluid oz. plain yogurt
1/2 C. kefir cheese
1 large cucumber
2 tbsp mint (dried and crushed)
2 tbsp basil (fresh finely chopped)
1 tsp onion powder (optional)
2 tbsp dried rose petals (optional)
1/2 C. walnuts (crushed) (optional)
1/2 C. raisins (optional)
salt
1 tbsp black pepper, to taste

Directions

1. Get a large mixing bowl: Combine in it the yogurt and kefir cheese. Mix them well.
2. Peel the cucumbers and chop them finely. Stir in the basil, mint, salt, pepper, onion powder, raisins, walnuts, and dried rose petals. Place it in the fridge until ready to serve.
3. Enjoy.

Persian Rosy Rice Pudding

Prep Time: 2 mins
Total Time: 42 mins

Servings per Recipe: 4
Calories	1846.8
Fat	1.4g
Cholesterol	0.0mg
Sodium	5.1mg
Carbohydrates	443.9g
Protein	16.1g

Ingredients

- 500 g rice
- 1 kg sugar
- cooking oil
- 1/2 tsp saffron
- 1/2 C. rose water
- pistachios, crushed
- almonds, crushed
- 1 tsp cinnamon

Directions

1. Rinse the rice with some water and drain it.
2. Place a large pot over medium heat. Place in it the rice and cover it with 6 times the amount of rice in water. Cook the rice until it is done.
3. Stir in the sugar until it completely melts.
4. Pour half C. of water in a small bowl. Stir in it the saffron then add it to the pot.
5. Pour the oil in a small saucepan. Heat it through and add it to the pot. Stir in the rosewater with almonds.
6. Lower the heat and cook the rice pudding for 30 min. Serve it warm with your favorite toppings.
7. Enjoy.

FENUGREEK
Lamb Stew

Prep Time: 20 mins
Total Time: 2 hrs 50 mins

Servings per Recipe: 6
Calories   356.9
Fat   20.4g
Cholesterol   98.4mg
Sodium   207.4mg
Carbohydrates   9.0g
Protein   33.2g

Ingredients

2 lbs boneless lamb stewing meat (cut into 3/4-inch cubes) or 2 lbs boneless beef roast (cut into 3/4-inch cubes)
1 large onion, finely chopped
1/3 C. cooking oil
1 tsp turmeric
1 1/2 C. water
6 dried limes or 1/2 C. fresh lime juice
3/4 C. kidney bean
1 large potato, diced (optional)

salt
black pepper
1 C. green onion, finely chopped
1 1/2 C. spinach, finely chopped
1/2 C. parsley, finely chopped
1/4 C. cilantro, finely chopped (optional)
1/4 C. garlic chives, finely chopped
1/4 C. fenugreek seeds, finely chopped (optional)

Directions

1. Discard the excess fat for the lamb and cut it into dices.
2. Place a large pan over medium heat. Heat in it half of the oil. Sauté in it the onion for 3 min. Add the lamb dices and cook them for 2 min.
3. Lower the heat then stir in the water, drained kidney beans, salt and pepper. Put on the lid and cook them for 1 h 10 min.
4. Place a large skillet over medium heat. Heat the rest of the oil in it. Add the potato and cook it until it becomes golden brown.
5. Drain the potato and stir it into the stew. Put on the lid and cook them for 12 min.
6. Add the remaining veggies into the same skillet and cook them for 4 min. Stir the mix with dry lime into the stew.
7. Put on the lid and cook the stew for 14 min. Serve it warm.
8. Enjoy.

Persian Cinnamon Beef Stew

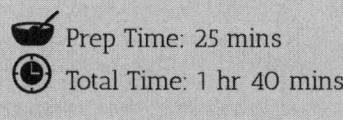

Prep Time: 25 mins
Total Time: 1 hr 40 mins

Servings per Recipe: 4	
Calories	425.1
Fat	24.3g
Cholesterol	82.9mg
Sodium	388.7mg
Carbohydrates	21.3g
Protein	30.0g

Ingredients

- 3 tbsp olive oil, divided (2 tbsp. and 1 tbsp.)
- 1/2 large onion, chopped
- 1 lb lean stewing beef, cubed
- 2 tsp ground cumin
- 2 tsp ground turmeric
- 1/2 tsp ground cinnamon
- 2 1/2 C. water
- 5 tbsp fresh flat-leaf parsley, chopped
- 3 tbsp snipped chives
- 1 (15 oz.) cans kidney beans, drained and rinsed
- 1 lemon, juice of
- 1 tbsp flour
- salt and black pepper

Directions

1. Place a large pan over medium heat. Heat 2 tbsp of olive oil in it. Brown in it the stew meat for 12 min.
2. Stir in the cumin, turmeric and cinnamon. Cook them for 2 min. Pour in the water and cook them until they start boiling.
3. Put on the lid and cook them for 48 min while stirring from to time.
4. Place a small skillet over medium heat. Heat 1 tbsp of oil in it. Add the parsley with chives. Cook them for 3 min. Stir them into the beef stew with beans and lemon juice.
5. Sprinkle some salt and pepper on the stew then add to it 1 tbsp of flour. Cook the stew for 35 min until it thickens. Serve it warm.
6. Enjoy.

PERSIAN
Lemon Kabobs

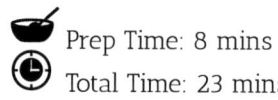
Prep Time: 8 mins
Total Time: 23 mins

Servings per Recipe: 12
Calories	94.9
Fat	5.8g
Cholesterol	25.7mg
Sodium	235.6mg
Carbohydrates	2.7g
Protein	7.4g

Ingredients

1 lb ground beef or 1 lb lamb
1 medium onion, grated
1/4 C. breadcrumbs or 1/4 C. white flour
1 egg, slightly beaten (optional)
1 tsp turmeric
1 tsp salt
1/2 tsp pepper
1 tbsp lemon juice

Directions

1. Squeeze the onion for the liquid. Transfer it to a large mixing bowl with the rest of the ingredients. Mix them well and place them in the fridge.
2. Preheat a grill and grease its grates.
3. Shape the mix into 10 or 12 patties. Press them into skewers to make logs. Cook the kabobs on the grill for 6 to 8 min on each side. Serve them warm.
4. Enjoy.

Persian Potato Lamb Stew

Prep Time: 30 mins
Total Time: 1 hr 30 mins

Servings per Recipe: 4
Calories   551.6
Fat   23.8g
Cholesterol   90.5mg
Sodium   1341.5mg
Carbohydrates   64.1g
Protein   25.8g

Ingredients

1 lb lamb, cut in cubes (or beef)
1/4 C. butter
1 lb green beans, cut in one-inch pieces
1 C. tomato paste
1 lb carrot, cut in one-inch slices
2 large waxy potatoes, cut in one-inch cubes
1/2 tsp cinnamon
1 tsp salt
1/4 tsp black pepper
1 tsp turmeric

Directions

1. Season the lamb meat with cinnamon.
2. Place a large pan over medium heat. Melt the butter in it. Cook in it the meat in batches for 5 min per batch. Stir in 2 C. of water.
3. Cook them until they start boiling. Lower the heat and cook them for 38 min with the lid on. Stir in the green beans, tomato paste, carrots, potatoes and spices.
4. Cook them for 38 min with the lid on. Adjust the seasoning of the stew then serve it warm.
5. Enjoy.

PERSIAN
Allspice Fish Fillets

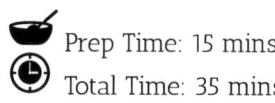

Prep Time: 15 mins
Total Time: 35 mins

Servings per Recipe: 3
Calories 289.7
Fat 2.2g
Cholesterol 132.0mg
Sodium 302.8mg
Carbohydrates 10.0g
Protein 56.0g

Ingredients

1/8 C. pomegranate molasses
1/3 C. water
1/2 C. tomato juice
1 lemon, juice of
1/2 tsp lemon zest
1/8 C. freshly squeezed lime juice
sea salt, to taste
1/8 tsp cumin
1/8 tsp cinnamon

1/8 tsp ground cardamom
couple pinches allspice
1/2 tbsp honey
olive oil
1/2 bunch scallion, chopped
1 garlic clove, crushed
4 fish fillets
gluten-free flour, mix

Directions

1. Get a small mixing bowl: Whisk in it the pomegranate molasses and water, tomato juice, lemon juice and zest, lime juice, sea salt, spices, and honey.
2. Place a large saucepan over medium heat. Heat 2 tbsp of olive oil in it. Sauté in it the garlic with scallions. Cook them for 3 min.
3. Stir in the molasses mix. Cook them until it starts boiling. Cook them for 4 min. Place the mix aside to make the sauce.
4. Before you do anything preheat the oven to 450 F.
5. Season the fish fillets with some salt. Dust the flour with them.
6. Place a large skillet over medium heat. Heat a splash of oil in it. Cook in it the fish fillets until they becomes golden brown for 3 to 6 min on each side.
7. Lay the fish fillets in a greased baking dish. Drizzle the sauce all over them. Cook them in the oven for 10 min. Serve your fish warm.
8. Enjoy.

Persian Meaty Okra Lime Stew

🥣 Prep Time: 15 mins
🕐 Total Time: 1 hr 30 mins

Servings per Recipe: 4
Calories   400.7
Fat   12.2g
Cholesterol   147.4mg
Sodium   259.5mg
Carbohydrates   22.3g
Protein   50.7g

Ingredients

- 1 1/2 lbs fresh okra
- 2 - 3 garlic cloves, sliced
- 2 lbs stewing lamb or 2 lbs beef, cut into small pieces
- 1 lb potato (optional)
- 2 large onions, sliced
- 2 - 3 tbsp fresh lime juice
- 3 - 4 tbsp tomato paste
- cooking oil
- salt and black pepper

Directions

1. Cut the onion into thin slices.
2. Place a large pan over medium heat. Heat a splash of oil in it. Add the onion and cook it until it becomes golden. Add the lamb dices with garlic.
3. Cook them for 3 min. Stir 3 C. of hot water. Cook them until they start boiling. Lower the heat and put on the lid. Cook them for 48 min.
4. Clean the okra and discard its stems. Add it to the pan with tomato paste, a pinch of salt and pepper. Put on the lid and cook it for 16 min without stirring.
5. Stir in the lime juice. Adjust the seasoning of the stew then serve it warm.
6. Enjoy.

PERSIAN Basmati Chicken Casserole

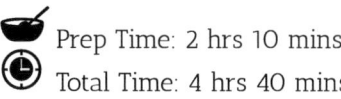
Prep Time: 2 hrs 10 mins
Total Time: 4 hrs 40 mins

Servings per Recipe: 4
Calories 865.3
Fat 29.9g
Cholesterol 259.5mg
Sodium 183.4mg
Carbohydrates 101.6g
Protein 44.8g

Ingredients

1 (2 1/4 lb) whole chicken
1 lb basmati rice
10 oz. plain nonfat yogurt
1/2 tsp saffron
2 large onions
3 egg yolks
cooking oil
salt (to taste)
black pepper (to taste)

Directions

1. Get a large bowl: Place in it the rice and cover it with warm water. Place it aside for 2 h 15 min.
2. Cut the chicken into pieces. Discard its skin. Peel the onion and chop it.
3. Place a large pan over medium heat. Heat a splash of oil in it. Sauté in it the onion for 3 min. Add the chicken and brown it.
4. Stir in some water and cook them until they start boiling. Lower the heat and cook them until the chicken is done while adding water if needed. Shred it
5. Get a large mixing bowl: Pour in it the yogurt. Beat it until it becomes creamy. Place it aside.
6. Get half C. of hot water. Stir in it the saffron until it dissolves. Add it to the yogurt with salt, pepper and egg yolks. Combine them well.
7. Cook the rice according to the directions on the package.
8. Before you do anything preheat the oven to 250 F.
9. Coat the bottom of a dutch oven with 3 tbsp of vegetable oil. Spread in it a thin layer of the yogurt mix followed by a thin layer of rice, chicken, another layer of rice and yogurt.
10. Repeat the process to make several other layers. Place the pot in the oven and cook it for 1 h 50 min.
11. Serve your chicken rice casserole warm.
12. Enjoy.

Persian Lemon Linguini

Prep Time: 20 mins
Total Time: 35 mins

Servings per Recipe: 4	
Calories	816.4
Fat	33.4g
Cholesterol	53.6mg
Sodium	812.7mg
Carbohydrates	99.4g
Protein	28.9g

Ingredients

- 500 g linguine
- 2 garlic cloves, peeled
- 2 tsp lemon rind, finely grated
- 1 bunch fresh basil, leaves picked
- 1/3 C. olive oil
- 3 anchovy fillets
- flaked sea salt
- black pepper, freshly ground
- 1/4 C. lemon juice
- 1/2 C. parmesan cheese, finely grated
- 2 egg tomatoes, finely chopped
- 180 g feta, drained, crumbled

Directions

1. Prepare the pasta by following the instructions on the package.
2. Get a mortar: Combine in it the garlic, lemon rind, half the basil and half the oil. Crush them with the pestle. Combine in the anchovies with the rest of basil.
3. Crush them again with the pestle. Stir in a pinch of salt and pepper.
4. Get a large mixing bowl: Toss in it the pasta with garlic mix, lemon juice and parmesan. Stir in the feta with tomato. Serve your pasta warm.
5. Enjoy.

PERSIAN
Herbed Rice

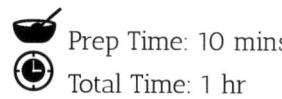

Prep Time: 10 mins
Total Time: 1 hr

Servings per Recipe: 8
Calories   342.5
Fat   9.9g
Cholesterol   20.3mg
Sodium   89.8mg
Carbohydrates   57.2g
Protein   6.8g

Ingredients

3 C. long grain white basmati rice
2 bunches green onions, minced
1 C. fresh dill weed, finely chopped
1 C. fresh parsley, finely chopped

1 C. fresh cilantro, finely chopped
1/3 C. butter

Directions

1. Get a large bowl: Place in it the rice and cover it with warm water. Place it aside for 2 h 15 min.
2. Fill half a large pot with water and a pinch of salt. Cook it until it starts boiling. Add the rice and cook it until it starts boiling.
3. Keep cooking it for 9 min. Strain the rice and place it aside to drain.
4. Get a food processor: Combine the scallions, dill, parsley and cilantro. Process them until they becomes smooth.
5. Melt the butter in a large pot over medium heat. Lay in it 1/3 of the cooked rice followed by half of the herbs mix. Repeat the process to make 2 other layers.
6. Make 5 holes with the spatula handle in the rice. Place a piece of foil over the pot and place the lid on it. Place it over medium heat and cook it for 4 min.
7. Lower the heat and cook it for 38 min. Place it aside for 16 min to rest. Serve it warm.
8. Enjoy.

Persian Kashk Lamb Meatballs Stew

Prep Time: 15 mins
Total Time: 1 hr 5 mins

Servings per Recipe: 4
Calories   467.9
Fat   18.0g
Cholesterol   45.6mg
Sodium   324.7mg
Carbohydrates   53.2g
Protein   33.7g

Ingredients

- 250 g ground lamb or 250 g beef
- 50 g dried black-eye beans
- 50 g dried split peas
- 50 g dried brown lentils
- 1 kg fresh spinach
- 2 onions
- 100 g of fresh mint
- 1/4 tsp pomegranate powder
- 1 C. kashk
- vegetable oil
- salt
- black pepper

Directions

1. Rinse the black-eye beans, split-peas, and lentils. Place them in a large bowl and cover them with water. Place them aside to soak for 4 h 10 min.
2. Rinse them and drain them. Place them in large saucepan with 4 1/4 C. of water with a pinch of salt. Cook them for 22 min over medium heat until 1 C. of liquid is left.
3. Get a large mixing bowl: Grate the onion and add to it the lamb with a pinch of salt and pepper. Mix them well. Shape the mix into meatballs.
4. Place a large pan over medium heat. Heat a splash of oil in it. Brown in it the meatballs for 4 min.
5. Rinse the spinach with some cool water and chop them. Stir them into the saucepan with the beans mix and meatballs. Cook them for 18 min. Stir in the pomegranate powder.
6. Place a small skillet over medium heat. Heat a splash of oil in it. Add the mint and fry it. Crush it and use it to garnish the stew. Serve it warm.
7. Enjoy.

PERSIAN
Sesame Bread

 Prep Time: 1 hr 30 mins
Total Time: 1 hr 45 mins

Servings per Recipe: 1
Calories   2450.9
Fat   61.9g
Cholesterol   0.0mg
Sodium   2372.2mg
Carbohydrates   410.2g
Protein   58.9g

Ingredients

500 g flour
40 g fresh yeast
250 - 275 ml warm water
1 tbsp brown sugar
1 tsp salt

4 tbsp olive oil
2 tbsp corn flour (optional)
1 tsp black sesame

Directions

1. Get a large mixing bowl: Mix in it the flour with corn flour and a pinch of salt. Mix them well.
2. Make a small well in the middle of the flour mix. Place in it the sugar with yeast and 5 tbsp of warm water Mix them well. Place it a side with a kitchen towel to cover it for 28 min.
3. Add the rest of the water and water then mix them again until you get a smooth dough. Place it aside to rest for 1 h 10 min.
4. Before you do anything preheat the oven to 400 F.
5. Shape the dough into several circles of flat bread and place them on lined up baking sheet. Brush them with olive oil and top them with sesame seeds.
6. Cook them in the oven for 15 to 18 min. Serve it warm or cold.
7. Enjoy.

Persian Kings' Almond Lamb Stew

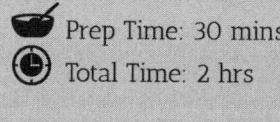

Prep Time: 30 mins
Total Time: 2 hrs

Servings per Recipe: 6
Calories 0.0
Fat 0.0g
Cholesterol 0.0mg
Sodium 0.0mg
Carbohydrates 0.0g
Protein 0.0g

Ingredients

- 8 garlic cloves, peeled
- 1 piece gingerroot, 2 . 5 cm cube (peeled & coarsely chopped)
- 50 g blanched almonds, slivered
- 6 tbsp water
- 7 tbsp vegetable oil
- 1 kg boneless lamb shoulder (In 2.5 cm cubes)
- 10 cardamom pods, 10 pieces
- 6 cloves
- 1 cinnamon stick, 3 cm long piece
- 200 g brown onions, finely chopped
- 1 tsp ground coriander
- 2 tsp ground cumin
- 1/2 tsp cayenne pepper
- 1 1/4 tsp salt
- 300 ml single cream
- 1/2 tsp garam masala

Directions

1. Get a food processor: Combine in it garlic, ginger and almonds and 6 tbsp of water. Blend them smooth.
2. Place a large pan over medium heat. Heat the oil in it. Brown in it the lamb in batches. Drain them and place them aside.
3. Add the cardamom, cloves and cinnamon to the pan. Cook them for 1 min. Add the onion and cook them for 4 min.
4. Lower the heat and add the garlic mix with coriander, cumin and cayenne. Cook them for 5 min. Toss in the browed lamb with cream, and 1/2 C. of water.
5. Cook them until they start boiling. Put on the lid and cook them over low heat for 1 h 35 min. While stirring often and adding water if needed.
6. Stir in the garam masala. Serve your stew warm.
7. Enjoy.

CHICKEN
Apricots Stir Fry

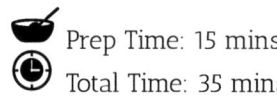
Prep Time: 15 mins
Total Time: 35 mins

Servings per Recipe: 4
Calories 588.6
Fat 27.1g
Cholesterol 72.6mg
Sodium 398.9mg
Carbohydrates 59.9g
Protein 33.6g

Ingredients

1 lb chicken breast, cut into 2 inch cubes
oil (for frying)
4 large portabella mushrooms, cut into 2 inch cubes
4 oz. dried apricots, coarsely chopped
1 C. cashews
3/4 C. raisins
salt and pepper
1/2 C. chicken broth
1 tbsp brown sugar
2 tsp sweet paprika
1/2 tsp ground ginger

Directions

1. Place a large pan over medium heat. Heat a splash of oil in it. Add the chicken and brown it for 5 min.
2. Stir in the mushroom and cook them for 3 min. Stir in the apricots, raisins, brown sugar, paprika, ginger, and salt and pepper. Cook them for 1 min 4 min.
3. Stir in the broth and cook them for 6 min over high heat. Fold in the cashews. Serve your stir fry with some rice.
4. Enjoy.

Persian Potato Frittata

🥣 Prep Time: 25 mins
🕐 Total Time: 1 hr 25 mins

Servings per Recipe: 6
Calories   276.5
Fat   10.9g
Cholesterol   70.5mg
Sodium   36.6mg
Carbohydrates   39.1g
Protein   6.5g

Ingredients

6 -7 potatoes, peeled and shredded
1 onion, shredded
2 eggs
mint
salt
pepper
turmeric
margarine
1/4 C. vegetable oil

Directions

1. Before you do anything preheat the oven to 400 F. Greased a casserole dish with some butter.
2. Get a large mixing bowl: Mix in it the potatoes, onion, eggs, salt, pepper, turmeric, mint.
3. Pour the vegetable oil over medium heat. Heat until it starts sizzling.
4. Pour the potato mix into the casserole dish. Drizzle the hot oil all over it. Place it in the oven and cook it for 1 10 min. Serve it warm.
5. Enjoy.

PERSIAN
Cinnamon Basmati Pilaf

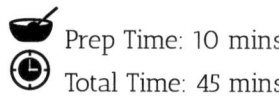

Prep Time: 10 mins
Total Time: 45 mins

Servings per Recipe: 6
Calories 319.8
Fat 10.5g
Cholesterol 10.1mg
Sodium 608.0mg
Carbohydrates 49.1g
Protein 8.6g

Ingredients

2 tbsp butter
1 small onion, chopped
1/2 C. slivered almonds
1 1/2 C. uncooked basmati rice
1/2 C. golden raisin
1 1/2 tsp ground turmeric
1/4 tsp cinnamon
1/2 tsp salt
3 C. chicken broth

Directions

1. Place a large pan over medium heat. Melt the butter in it. Sauté in it the onion with almonds for 8 min over high heat.
2. Add the rice with raisins, turmeric, cinnamon and a pinch of salt. Cook them for 3 min. Stir in the broth. Cook them until they start boiling.
3. Put on the lid and lower the heat. Cook the pilaf for 26 min. Serve it warm.
4. Enjoy.

Persian Walnuts Cake

Prep Time: 10 mins
Total Time: 35 mins

Servings per Recipe: 16
Calories	344.2
Fat	19.9g
Cholesterol	30.5mg
Sodium	2.7mg
Carbohydrates	41.0g
Protein	4.8g

Ingredients

- 3 C. pitted dates
- 1 C. walnuts, coarsely chopped
- DOUGH
- 1 C. unsalted butter
- 1 1/2 C. sifted all-purpose flour
- 1/2 C. powdered sugar
- 1 tsp ground cinnamon
- 1/2 tsp ground cardamom
- 1 C. pistachios, ground unsalted or 1 C. coconut, shredded

Directions

1. Place a large skillet. Toasted in it the walnuts for 6 min. Place them aside.
2. Place some walnuts in the middle of the dates. Lay them in the bottom of a serving dish.
3. Place a large pan over medium heat. Cook in it the four with butter for 18 min until they becomes golden brown over high heat.
4. Pour the hot mix all over the dates and spread it.
5. Get a small mixing bowl: Mix in it the cinnamon, sugar, cardamom. Sprinkle the mix all over the butter and flour layer followed by the pistachios. Place the cake aside to lose heat.
6. Serve it with your favorite toppings.
7. Enjoy.

PERSIAN
Valentine Almond Cake

Prep Time: 15 mins
Total Time: 50 mins

Servings per Recipe: 8
Calories 559.2
Fat 33.1g
Cholesterol 78.7mg
Sodium 318.6mg
Carbohydrates 61.4g
Protein 10.1g

Ingredients

3 C. almond meal
1 C. raw sugar
1 C. brown sugar
1 tsp salt
120 g unsalted butter, softened
2 eggs, lightly beaten
250 g Greek yogurt, plus extra to serve
4 tsp freshly grated nutmeg
1/4 C. pistachio nut, coarsely chopped

Directions

1. Before you do anything preheat the oven to 356 F. Lined up and grease a spring form pan with butter.
2. Get a large mixing bowl: Mix in it the almond meal, sugars, butter and salt. Knead it with your hands until it becomes crumbled.
3. Spread half of the mix in the greased baking dish. Press it with your hands.
4. Get a large mixing bowl: Combine the rest of the almond meal mix with the egg, yogurt and nutmeg. Mix them well. Spoon the mix over the almond meal mix layer. Top it with pistachios.
5. Cook it in the oven for 34 min. Place the cake aside until it loses heat completely. Serve it with your favorite toppings.
6. Enjoy.

Persian Basmati Prunes Soup

🥣 Prep Time: 1 hr
🕐 Total Time: 2 hrs

Servings per Recipe: 4
Calories   328.7
Fat   15.5g
Cholesterol   45.6mg
Sodium   44.6mg
Carbohydrates   33.3g
Protein   13.9g

Ingredients

- 100 g basmati rice or 100 g long-grain rice
- 500 g herbs (parsley, mint, coriander, spring-onion ends)
- 250 g ground lamb or 250 g beef
- 300 g pitted prunes
- 4 large onions
- cooking oil
- salt
- black pepper

Directions

1. Get a large mixing bowl: Place in it the prunes and cover them with warm water. Place them aside for 2 h 15 min to soften.
2. Place a large saucepan over medium heat. Heat a splash of oil in it. Slice the onion and cook it in it until it becomes golden.
3. Add the lamb meat and cook them for 5 min. Stir in 4 C. of water. Cook them until they start boiling.
4. Chop the herbs finely. Stir the with the prunes and rice into the saucepan with a pinch of salt and pepper. Cook them for 22 min or until the rice is done while adding water if needed.
5. Serve your soup warm.
6. Enjoy.

PERSIAN
Orangy Nuts Soup

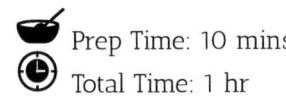
Prep Time: 10 mins
Total Time: 1 hr

Servings per Recipe: 4
Calories   334.7
Fat   21.0g
Cholesterol   0.0mg
Sodium   1732.1mg
Carbohydrates   23.5g
Protein   15.5g

Ingredients

1 C. pistachios, shelled
1 - 2 tbsp olive oil
1 shallot, diced finely
1 leek, chopped finely
1 garlic clove, minced
3 tbsp rice flour
6 C. chicken broth or 6 C. stock

1 tsp salt
1/4 tsp pepper or 1/4 tsp white pepper
1/4 C. orange juice
2 tbsp lime juice or 2 tbsp lemon juice
2 tbsp pistachios, slivered (garnish)

Directions

1. Rinse the pistachios and soak them for several minutes. Transfer them to a food processor and process them until they becomes smooth.
2. Place a large saucepan over medium heat. Heat the oil in it. Add the shallot, leek and the garlic. Cook them for 3 min.
3. Stir in the rice flour. Pour in the broth while stirring. Cook them until they start boiling. Stir in the ground pistachios, salt, and pepper.
4. Lower the heat and put on the lid. Cook the soup for 48 min. Add the orange and lime/lemon juices. Adjust the seasoning of the soup then serve it warm.
5. Enjoy.

Persian Yogurt Beef Soup

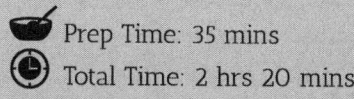

Prep Time: 35 mins
Total Time: 2 hrs 20 mins

Servings per Recipe: 6
Calories   605.8
Fat   30.0g
Cholesterol   186.0mg
Sodium   281.3mg
Carbohydrates   41.3g
Protein   40.4g

Ingredients

- 2 lbs ground beef
- 2 eggs
- 1/2 C. fresh parsley (Large Bunch, Chopped)
- 4 C. fresh spinach
- 1 onion, Medium, Chopped Finely
- 1 onion, Small, Grated
- 1/4 C. lentils (Uncooked)
- 1/4 C. kidney bean (Canned)
- 1 quart plain yogurt
- 1 C. uncooked rice,
- 1/2 tsp turmeric, for color
- 1 dash salt
- 1 dash pepper
- 1 quart water

Directions

1. Get a mixing bowl: Whisk in it the turmeric, Salt, Pepper, and Yogurt. Put on it the fridge.
2. Place a large pan over medium heat. Heat a splash of oil in it. Add the onion and cook it for 4 min.
3. Stir in the parsley, spinach, beans, and water while adding more to cover them if needed. Cook them for 1 h 10 min.
4. Get a large mixing bowl: Combine in it the Beef, Eggs, dash of Salt & Pepper, and Grated Onion. Mix them well. Shape the mix into meatballs.
5. Stir the rice with meatballs into the soup. Cook them for 32 min. Place the soup aside to lose heat for 16 min.
6. Ladle some of the liquid from the soup and add it to the yogurt mix. Whisk it well until it becomes smooth. Stir the mix into the soup.
7. Adjust the seasoning of the soup then serve it warm.
8. Enjoy.

PERSIAN
Garbanzo Soup

Prep Time: 15 mins
Total Time: 3 hrs 15 mins

Servings per Recipe: 8
Calories   184.7
Fat   1.3g
Cholesterol   0.0mg
Sodium   104.1mg
Carbohydrates   37.1g
Protein   8.7g

Ingredients

125 g pearl barley
750 g fresh herbs equal portions parsley, spinach, chive, dill and coriander
125 g garbanzo beans
125 g red kidney beans
125 g lentils
1/4 C. white rice
3 medium onions
2 C. kashk
1 tbsp dried mint
1 tsp turmeric
salt and pepper

Directions

1. Soak the beans for an overnight. Soak the barley with rice for an overnight.
2. Place the beans in a large pot. Cover them with water and cook them of 1 h 10 with lid on over low heat. Add the barely and rice. Cook them until they are done.
3. Chop them finely. Stir them into the pot. Cook them over low heat for 35 min while stirring often. Lower the heat and cook them for 2 h 10 min until everything is soft.
4. Turn off the heat. Stir in the kashk with a pinch of salt and pepper.
5. Place a large pan over medium heat. Heat a splash of oil in it. Sauté in it the onion after slicing it for 6 min. Serve it over the soup warm.
6. Enjoy.

Persian Lover's Rose Tea

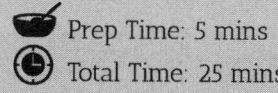
Prep Time: 5 mins
Total Time: 25 mins

Servings per Recipe: 4
Calories   24.6
Fat   0.0g
Cholesterol   0.0mg
Sodium   7.3mg
Carbohydrates   6.3g
Protein   0.0g

Ingredients

- 4 C. water
- 2 green cardamom pods, bruised
- 1/2 tsp saffron thread, ground
- 1/2 C. rose water
- 2 tbsp sugar

Directions

1. Place a kettle over medium heat. Combine in it the water, rose water, cardamom pods and sugar then stir them until the sugar melts.
2. Cook the tea until it starts boiling. Lower the heat and put on the lid. Cook the tea for 16 min. Discard the cardamom pods. Serve it warm.
3. Enjoy.

PERSIAN
Beef Pasta Sauce

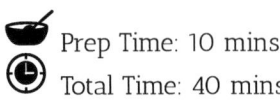 Prep Time: 10 mins
Total Time: 40 mins

Servings per Recipe: 4
Calories 357.4
Fat 24.1g 37
Cholesterol 77.1mg
Sodium 678.6mg
Carbohydrates 12.0g
Protein 23.5g

Ingredients

1 lb ground beef
1 large onion, finely chopped
1 large tomatoes, peeled, seeded, and chopped
2 - 3 garlic cloves, finely chopped
16 oz. tomato sauce
1/3 tsp turmeric
salt and pepper
1/2 C. water
2 tbsp oil

Directions

1. Place a large pan over medium heat. Heat 2 tbsp of oil in it. Add the onion and cook it for 3 min. Add the garlic and cook it for 2 min.
2. Stir in the turmeric and cook them for 1 min. Stir in the beef and cook them for 6 to 8 min until it browned. Discard the excess fat.
3. Stir n the tomato with tomato sauce, water, a pinch of salt and pepper. Put on the lid and cook the sauce for 35 min. Serve it warm.
4. Enjoy.

Persian Herbed Cucumber Cream Dip

🥘 Prep Time: 15 mins
🕐 Total Time: 1 hr 15 mins

Servings per Recipe: 1
Calories   219.0
Fat   12.3g
Cholesterol   31.0mg
Sodium   323.0mg
Carbohydrates   22.7g
Protein   7.3g

Ingredients

DIP
1 English cucumber, peeled and diced
1/2 C. raisins
3 C. whole milk yogurt, drained
1/2 C. sour cream
1/4 C. green onion, chopped
1 tbsp of fresh mint, chopped
2 tbsp fresh dill weed, chopped
2 garlic cloves, peeled and finely minced
3 tbsp walnuts, finely chopped

1/2 tsp salt, to taste
1/4 tsp black pepper
GARNISH
1/2 tsp of fresh mint
2 tbsp fresh rose petals, cut into ribbons
1 dried rose bud (optional)

Directions

1. Get a serving bowl: Mix in it the cucumber, raisins, yogurt, sour cream, scallions, mint, dill, garlic and walnuts. Season it with some salt and pepper.
2. Put on the lid and place the lid in the fridge for 1 h 10 min. Serve it with some mint and rose petals on top.
3. Enjoy.

CREAMY Roasted Persian Eggplant Lime Dip

Prep Time: 10 mins
Total Time: 50 mins

Servings per Recipe: 8
Calories 48.4
Fat 1.4g
Cholesterol 2.7mg
Sodium 303.2mg
Carbohydrates 8.2g
Protein 2.0g

Ingredients

2 (1 lb) large eggplants
1 tsp olive oil
4 cloves garlic, peeled and crushed
1 tsp salt
1/2 tsp fresh ground black pepper
2/3 C. drained yogurt
4 tsp of fresh mint, chopped or 1 tsp dried mint
2 tsp fresh lime juice

GARNISH
1/4 tsp powdered saffron, threads in (optional)
2 tsp hot water (optional)
1 tsp drained yogurt
fresh mint leaves

Directions

1. Before you do anything preheat the oven to 350 F. Pierce the eggplants several times with a fork. Place them in a baking sheet.
2. Cook them in the oven for 42 min until they becomes soft. Place them aside to lose heat. Peel the eggplants and finely chop them.
3. Get a large mixing bowl: Combine in the chopped eggplant with the rest of the ingredients Adjust the seasoning of the dip then serve it.
4. Enjoy

Creamy Persian Zesty Garlic Dip

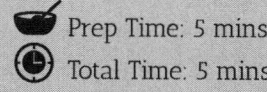

Prep Time: 5 mins
Total Time: 5 mins

Servings per Recipe: 1	
Calories	2006.5
Fat	216.3g
Cholesterol	0.0mg
Sodium	6991.2mg
Carbohydrates	22.4g
Protein	3.9g

Ingredients

- 20 garlic cloves
- 1 C. olive oil
- 1 tbsp salt
- 2 - 3 tbsp fresh lemon juice
- 1 dash cayenne

Directions

1. Get a food processor: Place in it the garlic and process it until it becomes finely chopped. Add the lemon juice with cayenne pepper. Mix them well.
2. Add the olive oil in a steady stream while blending all the time until they become smooth. Serve your dip.
3. Enjoy.

PERSIAN
Greek Dip

Prep Time: 5 mins
Total Time: 5 mins

Servings per Recipe: 4
Calories   37.9
Fat   0.1g
Cholesterol   1.2mg
Sodium   47.7mg
Carbohydrates   5.5g
Protein   3.6g

Ingredients

1 shallot
1 C. plain nonfat yogurt
1 C. Greek yogurt

Directions

1. Cut the shallot into dices.
2. Get a mixing bowl: Combine in it the shallot with the rest of the ingredients. Stir them well. Place the mix in the fridge for 2 h 30 min with the lid on.
3. Serve it with your favorite toppings.
4. Enjoy.

Grilled Persian Garlic and Eggplant Dip

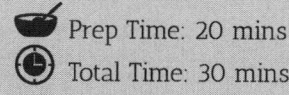

Prep Time: 20 mins
Total Time: 30 mins

Servings per Recipe: 2	
Calories	427.1
Fat	20.2g
Cholesterol	186.0mg
Sodium	92.9mg
Carbohydrates	55.9g
Protein	16.2g

Ingredients

- 4 eggplants
- 2 garlic cloves
- 2 eggs
- 1 tomatoes
- 2 tbsp oil
- salt
- black pepper

Directions

1. Preheat the grill and grease it.
2. Pierce the eggplants several times with a fork. Place them on the grill and cook them until they become soft.
3. Place the eggplants aside to lose heat. Pee them and chop them finely.
4. Place a large skillet over medium heat. Heat the oil in it. Add the garlic and cook it for 1 min. Stir in the tomato with eggplant, a pinch of salt and pepper. Cook them for 4 min.
5. Get a small bowl: Whisk in it the eggs. Add them to the pan and cook them for 3 min. Serve your dip warm.
6. Enjoy.

REFRESHING
Nutty Cucumber Cream Salad

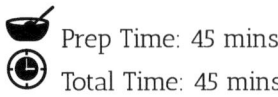

Prep Time: 45 mins
Total Time: 45 mins

Servings per Recipe: 4	
Calories	92.3
Fat	2.5g
Cholesterol	1.2mg
Sodium	50.3mg
Carbohydrates	13.8g
Protein	4.9g

Ingredients

- 1 English cucumber
- salt
- 1 C. nonfat plain yogurt
- 2 tbsp raisins, soaked in
- 2 tbsp water
- 2 tbsp walnuts, chopped
- 1 small onion, minced
- 1/4 tsp white pepper
- 1 tbsp chopped of fresh mint
- 1 pinch dried basil
- lettuce(to garnish)

Directions

1. Peel the cucumber. Cut 4 longs slices from its sides and place them aside. Slice the pulp middle of the cucumber thinly. place them aside in a shallow bowl.
2. Sprinkle some salt over the cucumber pulp slices. Place it aside for 35 min. Drain it and pat it dry.
3. Get a mixing bowl: Toss in the yogurt with the cucumber pulp slices. Stir in the rest of the ingredients. Serve your dip with the cucumber slices.
4. Enjoy.

ENJOY THE RECIPES?

KEEP ON COOKING WITH 6 MORE FREE COOKBOOKS!

Visit our website and simply enter your email address to join the club and receive your 6 cookbooks.

http://booksumo.com/magnet

https://www.instagram.com/booksumopress/

https://www.facebook.com/booksumo/

Printed in Great Britain
by Amazon